Bureau of Land Management

National Scenic and Historic Trails Strategy and Work Plan

Produced by
U.S. Department of the Interior
Bureau of Land Management
National Landscape Conservation System
National Scenic and Historic Trails Program
Washington, D.C.

I0450435

BLM

National Landscape Conservation System
Healthy, Wild, and Open

BLM-WO-GI-06-020-6250

Dear Reader

The Bureau of Land Management's (BLM) National Landscape Conservation System Office is pleased to provide you with the National Scenic and Historic Trails (NSHT) Strategy and Work Plan. The purpose of this national-level strategy is to provide a 10-year framework for the development of program guidance and direction for improved management of the BLM's NSHT Program. The strategy contains a mission statement, followed by a set of goals, objectives, and actions. The work plan outlines the priorities, timeframes, and responsible offices. The BLM expects to implement the strategy over the next 10 years, according to funding, staffing, and priorities. All work in the strategy is based on authorities in the Federal Land Management and Policy Act, the National Trails System Act, the National Historic Preservation Act, and other related law and policy.

The strategy focuses on improving the BLM's administrative oversight functions for this program, enhancing visitor services and recreation management, providing consistent direction for the protection and development of trail resources in a multiple-use environment, and advancing partnering with trail organizations and other agencies along these trails.

The BLM manages land along 2 national scenic trails and 10 national historic trails in 10 western States. The agency manages more miles of national historic trails than any other Federal agency. The Bureau is also the trail administrating agency for the Iditarod National Historic Trail in Alaska, and partners with the National Park Service in this role for the El Camino Real de Tierra Adentro and Old Spanish National Historic Trails across six southwestern States. The BLM also manages seven major trail-related visitor centers, often in partnership with State or local government agencies and interest groups.

The BLM appreciates the public comments received on the draft strategy from organizations, associations, industry, government agencies, and private citizens. The comments are reflected as appropriate in the direction contained in the final document. It is only through this diverse public participation that we can cooperatively effect positive change in our resource programs.

Recommended by:

Elena Daly, Director
National Landscape Conservation System Office
Bureau of Land Management

Approved by:

Kathleen Clarke, Director
Bureau of Land Management

Contents

The National Trails System Act passed in 1968, establishing the National Trails System. The Act states that "*In order to provide for the ever-increasing outdoor recreation needs of an expanding population and in order to promote the preservation of, public access to, travel within, and enjoyment and appreciation of the open-air, outdoor areas and historic resources of the Nation, trails should be established....*" The Bureau of Land Management (BLM) is entering the 37th year of managing and administering designated National Scenic and Historic Trails.

To date, the BLM manages land along 2 National Scenic Trails totaling 608 miles, and 10 National Historic Trails totaling 4,877 miles in 10 western States (Appendix B—BLM National Scenic and Historic Trails Mileage Table). The National Scenic Trails include the Pacific Crest and the Continental Divide, and the National Historic Trails include the Iditarod, Nez Perce, Mormon Pioneer, Lewis and Clark, Oregon, California, Juan Bautista de Anza, El Camino Real de Tierra Adentro, Old Spanish, and Pony Express. The BLM Eastern States Office is researching potential connections with the Potomac Heritage National Scenic Trail in Maryland and Virginia. On some additional national trails, the BLM may manage subsurface oil and gas or mineral leases, where the surface is managed by another agency or private entity. About 80 BLM Field Offices manage more miles of National Historic Trails than any other Federal agency, whereas about 15 offices work along the National Scenic Trails.

In addition, the Bureau administers (serves as lead agency for) the Iditarod National Historic Trail in Alaska, and collaborates with the National Park Service in this role for El Camino Real de Tierra Adentro and Old Spanish National Historic Trails. Trail administration includes coordinating all Federal, Tribal, State, and local governments, trail organizations, advisory councils, interested private landowners, land users, and other interested parties to plan and manage the trail (National Trails System Act). The National Park Service administers 17 National Scenic and Historic Trails, and the U.S. Forest Service administers 4.

The BLM also manages, comanages, or provides resources for seven major trail-related visitor centers, often in partnership with State or local agencies and groups. These centers are the El Camino Real International Heritage Center (New Mexico), Fort Benton (Montana), National Historic Trails Interpretive Center (Wyoming), National Historic Oregon Trail Interpretive Center (Oregon), Pompey's Pillar Interpretive Center, Sacajawea Interpretive Cultural and Education Center (Idaho), and the California Trails Interpretive Center (under development in Nevada).

Background

The Bureau's responsibility for managing and administering congressionally designated trails dates back to the passage of the National Trails System Act in 1968, which included the designation of Pacific Crest National Scenic Trail. This trail exists, in part, on BLM-managed land. In 1976, the Federal Land Policy and Management Act (FLPMA) referenced the National Trails System, reaffirming BLM's involvement with these trails. Agency responsibility increased with the designation of five more trails in 1978, and the scope of the work changed when the Department of the Interior named the BLM as trail administrator for the Iditarod National Historic Trail in Alaska. During the 1980s, one more trail was added. Three trails were added in the 1990s and four in the 2000s. To date, seven major trail-related visitor centers have been built or are under construction for these trails involving the BLM.

The BLM uses policy guidance from related laws, regulations, and policies for consistency in planning, mitigation, and other actions across the agency for these trails. One regulation exists for the Continental Divide National Scenic Trail regarding motorized use.

The Bureau participates as a member of the Federal Interagency Council on Trails, including the National Park Service, U.S. Forest Service, Federal Highway Administration, U.S. Fish and Wildlife Service, and others. The group presently operates under a

Memorandum of Understanding focusing on uniform implementation and a seamless interagency approach to management, where possible. The Bureau also maintains partnerships with approximately 16 National Scenic and Historic Trail organizations dedicated to the advocacy, preservation, and day-to-day care of these trails.

With the creation of the National Landscape Conservation System (NLCS) Office for oversight of Congressional and Presidential designations in 2000, BLM National Scenic and Historic Trails are now managed as one program. The NLCS Office works closely with the BLM recreation, cultural resources, and engineering groups, as well as others, to help ensure a consistent management approach.

Issues

The need for a strategy and work plan stems not only from the addition of new trails to the System, growing trail administration responsibilities, new visitor centers, and policy improvement, but also from a growing number of management issues in the field. These issues not only concern BLM staff and managers, but also trail organizations and other public land interests and users.

Recreational use is increasing significantly for some trails because of events such as the Lewis and Clark Bicentennial, reenactments, retracing, and recent trends in heritage tourism. Trail issues involve visitor use conflicts, sanitation, visitor centers, trail ethics, vegetation and soil loss, historic site vandalism, visitor health and safety, law enforcement, travel management, interpretation, and education. Concerns surface with partnership work, integration of visitor centers with trail administration and management, and with the high cost of construction and operation of visitor centers. Public issues arise with trail access, land acquisition, land disposal or exchange, easements, permitting, and trespass.

Improvements in planning, plan coordination, and mitigation are needed. This includes the statutorily required comprehensive trail management planning and agency land use and activity planning. It also includes the potential location and mitigation for new projects implemented within National Scenic and Historic Trail settings and viewsheds.

Partnerships with other agencies and trail organizations can create opportunities and challenges. These include roles, lines of authority, levels of involvement, training, volunteer care, tracking of volunteer time, job titles and position descriptions, partnership relations, agreements, and seamless management.

Last, funding is a basic and essential program component. Budget levels, tracking, accountability, justifications, workload measurement, staffing levels, staffing time, partner contributions, challenge cost-share, and other factors contribute to the stability of the National Scenic and Historic Trails Program in the agency and must be addressed.

Authority

This National Scenic and Historic Trails Strategy and Work Plan provides a framework for the development of program guidance and direction for BLM for the next 10 years.[1] The strategy and subsequent work will be based on existing laws, regulations, executive orders, agency policies, and departmental and agency strategic plans. These documents include the Federal Land Policy and Management Act, National Trails System Act, the National Historic Preservation Act and related laws, Executive Order 13195 "Trails for America in the 21st Century," the Department of the Interior's Strategic Plan, and the BLM's Priorities for Recreation and Visitor Services. The NLCS Office has developed this national strategy with input from various Bureau programs, agencies, trail organizations, and public land interests.

---

[1] Both scenic and historic trails are congressionally designated and share common objectives and purposes in the National Trails System Act. This strategy-level document therefore addresses them collectively. In work plan implementation, however, distinctions will be drawn between these two trail types, as appropriate.

This strategy and work plan will only guide the National Scenic and Historic Trails Program for the Bureau, not all components of the National Trails System Act. National Recreation Trails and the Rails to Trails Program are also included in the Act, but are outside the scope of this document because of differences in levels of designation, varying uses, purposes, complexity, processes, unique constituency groups, and relative size and mileage of the programs. These other trails may be addressed in the ongoing series of trail and travel management strategies by the BLM National Recreation Group, including such products as the National Management Strategy for Motorized Off-Highway Vehicle Use and the National Mountain Bicycling Strategic Action Plan.

Process

The basis of this strategy stems from work completed at a facilitated Bureau of Land Management National Scenic and Historic Trail Workshop held at the Mission Inn in Riverside, California, in March 2004. After the workshop, a core team of BLM trails program staff, assisted by a management advisory group, analyzed and compiled the workshop product into an initial Draft National Scenic and Historic Trails Strategy and Work Plan. The initial draft was reviewed internally, and comments were addressed and incorporated by the core team. The next draft was circulated for general public comment between April 29, 2005, and July 1, 2005. The comments received from that review are incorporated into this final document.

The following is the BLM National Scenic and Historic Trails Strategy, which will guide the Bureau in preparing its first programmatic direction for the management and administration of these trails. It contains the Statement of Policy and the related objectives and purposes from the National Trails System Act, the BLM's proposed Mission Statement for the National Scenic and Historic Trails Program, and goals, objectives, and actions that will guide the agency in developing a consistent approach to administering and managing these trails.

The need for the strategy includes improving the BLM's administrative oversight functions for this program, enhancing visitor services and recreation management, providing consistent direction for the protection and development of trail resources in a multiple-use environment, and advancing partnerships with trail organizations and other agencies along these trails.

Normal planning and work will continue on National Scenic and Historic Trails while this strategy is developed and implemented. In turn, advances in the national strategy will complement and benefit on-the-ground activities.

Statement of Policy from the National Trails System Act

"In order to provide for the ever-increasing outdoor recreation needs of an expanding population and in order to promote the preservation of, public access to, travel within, and enjoyment and appreciation of the open-air, outdoor areas and historic resources of the Nation, trails should be established (i) primarily, near the urban areas of the Nation, and (ii) secondarily, within scenic areas and along historic travel routes of the Nation which are often more remotely located.

"The purpose of this Act is to provide the means for obtaining these objectives by instituting a national system of recreation, scenic and historic trails, by designating the Appalachian Trail and the Pacific Crest Trail as the initial components of that system, and by prescribing the methods by which, and standards according to which, additional components may be added to the system.

"The Congress recognizes the valuable contributions that volunteers and private, nonprofit trail groups have made to the development and maintenance of the Nation's trails. In recognition of these contributions, it is further the purpose of this Act to encourage and assist volunteer citizen involvement in the planning, development, maintenance, and management, where appropriate, of trails."

Objectives, Purposes, and Definitions of the National Trails System Act

Objectives of the National Trails System Act

Section (a)
1. Provide for recreation needs
2. Promote preservation, public access, travel, enjoyment, and appreciation

Purposes of the National Trails System Act

Section (b)
1. Provide a means for attaining these objectives
2. Institute a national system
3. Prescribe methods and standards for adding components

Section (c)
1. Recognize contribution of volunteers and private, nonprofit trail groups
2. Encourage and assist volunteer citizen involvement, where appropriate

Definitions

National historic trails: follow as closely as possible and practicable the original trails or routes of travel of national historic significance...[and]...shall have as their purpose the identification and protection of the historic route and its historic remnants and artifacts for public use and enjoyment (National Trails System Act).

National scenic trails: so located as to provide for maximum outdoor recreation potential and for the conservation and enjoyment of the nationally significant scenic, historic, natural, or cultural qualities of the areas through which such trails may pass (National Trails System Act).

Mission Statement

"The mission of the BLM National Scenic and Historic Trails Program is to connect people to the land and its scenic wonders, our heritage, our cultures, and our communities. Through partnerships, community involvement, citizen action and agency commitment, the BLM will administer and manage the diverse network of Congressionally-designated trails and associated landscapes. In order to provide for enriching and inspiring experiences, the BLM, in fulfilling our multiple-use mandate, will protect and sustain trail resources while fostering visitor enjoyment, appreciation, and learning opportunities."

Goals

Four strategy goals were derived from the mission statement. After each goal is the excerpt used as the basis for its development:

Administrative Goal: Institute and formalize the National Scenic and Historic Trails Program within the BLM pursuant to the National Trails System Act and our multiple-use mandate.

"The BLM will administer and manage the diverse network of Congressionally-designated trails and associated landscapes."

Resource Goal: Protect and sustain trail resources to provide for enriching and inspiring experiences, scenic landscapes, or historic settings.

"In order to provide for enriching and inspiring experiences, the BLM, in fulfilling our multiple-use mandate, will protect and sustain trail resources."

Partnership Goal: Engage and encourage partnership involvement in planning, development, maintenance, and management, where appropriate.

"Through partnerships, community involvement, citizen action, and agency commitment, the BLM will administer and manage the diverse network of Congressionally-designated trails and associated landscapes."

Visitor Goal: Promote appropriate public access and foster visitor enjoyment, appreciation, and learning opportunities to provide for enriching and inspiring experiences.

"In order to provide for enriching and inspiring experiences, the BLM will foster visitor enjoyment, appreciation, and learning opportunities."

Administrative Goal

Institute and formalize the National Scenic and Historic Trails Program within the BLM pursuant to the National Trails System Act and our multiple-use mandate.

Objective 1: Establish an administrative infrastructure focusing on National Scenic and Historic Trails in the Bureau.

Rationale: In order to institutionalize the National Scenic and Historic Trails Program in accordance with congressional intent and pursuant to the mandates of the National Trails System Act, this objective creates and refines roles within the BLM's organization. Implementation will result in coordinated and consistent approaches, cost efficiencies, and reduction of management conflicts.

Actions:

1. Assess Workforce. Assess workforce needs and develop a table of organization for the BLM National Scenic and Historic Trails Program, including roles and responsibilities in the National, State, District, and Field Office levels. Consider other agency structures.

- Create administrative structure. Define the roles and responsibilities of State and Field Offices in planning, administration, and management of national scenic and national historic trails. Assess the need for additional staff (e.g., Trail Liaison for each trail).

- Clarify roles and relationships and increase coordination among the following: Trail Administrators (Managers), Trail Liaisons, Primary State Office Contacts, Primary Field Office Contacts, Visitor Center Contacts, Washington Office Contacts (NLCS, Cultural, Engineering, and Recreation).

2. Establish Trail Expert Team. Develop workgroup of trail experts and master performers who have knowledge and experience covering the specific aspects of National Scenic and Historic Trails.

- Develop a list of expertise needed and individuals with that expertise through local, State, Tribal, and Federal government, organizations, individuals, and industry.

- Make the contact list with associated expertise available to all the trail managers and partners.

3. Examine Visitor–Interpretive Centers' Roles. In cooperation with affected BLM programs, define the BLM's role in trail-related visitor centers as a component of best management practices, including use and support of existing visitor centers. With consideration to changing budget priorities, evaluate circumstances, implications, and consider alternatives to additional centers.

Objective 2: Establish budget structure and improve funding stream for National Scenic and Historic Trails in the Bureau.

Rationale: In order to ensure adequate funding to properly protect congressionally recognized national trail resources and monitor success, this objective eliminates conflict of purpose and will provide a mechanism to improve funding and identify and track use of designated funds.

Actions:

1. Propose Need for Subactivity Account. Evaluate a new subactivity account for National Scenic and Historic Trails protection work and activities on BLM lands.

2. Propose Budget Themes for Budget Planning System (BPS). Consider separate themes for National Scenic and Historic Trails apart from budget themes for associated visitor centers. Consider theme to use innovative methods to enhance visitor services without increases in budget. Work with Recreation, Engineering, and Cultural programs to ensure that life-cycle costs of visitor centers and other factors are considered in funding.

3. **Evaluate Need to Earmark Challenge Cost-Share (CCS) Themes for Funding Allocations.** Evaluate the need to earmark CCS funds for National Trail System work with partners.

4. **Create Project Codes.** Identify a separate trail-specific project code for each BLM National Scenic and Historic Trail for expenditure and accomplishment tracking, as well as budget and accomplishment planning.

5. **Refine Performance Measures.** Refine Program Elements, performance measures, and reporting requirements for National Scenic and Historic Trails for long-term management, assessment, and evaluation.

Objective 3: Clarify and open communication channels within the administrative structure.

Rationale: Improved communication will facilitate ownership and appreciation of the National Scenic and Historic Trails within the agency. An established communication network will result in enhanced internal and external program coordination.

Actions:

1. **Develop an Internal Communication Plan.** Develop a communication plan to enhance information transfer within BLM regarding National Scenic and Historic Trails (NLCS, Cultural, Engineering, and Recreation, and others). Ensure consistency with communication plan associated with the Partnership Goal.

Resource Goal

Protect and sustain trail resources to provide for enriching and inspiring experiences, scenic landscapes, or historic settings.

Objective 1: Establish and implement national policy and guidance to identify and protect trail resources in conjunction with our multiple-use mandate.

Rationale: Consistent guidance and need-specific training will provide the management tools and knowledge necessary to make informed and consistent decisions to protect and sustain trail resources for the public benefit.

Actions:

1. Reconnect Legislation to Contemporary Action. Create a legislative history of the National Trails System Act, subsequent legislation, and Executive Order. From this, produce a plain language guide for use by agencies and the public. Coordinate with interested partners.

2. Conduct Policy Review. Review existing policies to determine adequacy for trail administration and trail management and any inherent conflicts. Collaborate with other agencies, such as the National Park Service, U.S. Forest Service, and State Historic Preservation Offices.

3. Consider Additional Regulations. Evaluate and determine the need for additional regulations for the administration and management of the National Trail System where BLM has the authority under the National Trail System Act. If needed, promulgate regulations.

4. Develop National Register Bulletin. Recommend to the Department that a National Register Bulletin be developed to provide guidance for the inventory, assessment, and evaluation of the integrity of both the National Historic Trail and its setting (e.g., surrounding landscape).

5. Develop Manuals or Handbooks. Develop a series of BLM manuals or handbooks that would address resource assessment, protection, and proper utilization of the National Scenic and Historic Trails. Documents would emphasize and expand proper trail management, address on-the-ground information, reference appropriate existing handbooks, and provide guidance. Topics to be considered would include:

- Working definitions that clarify unique features and differences between National Scenic Trails and National Historic Trails

- Inventory and condition assessment

- Deferred and annual maintenance

- Monitoring

- Capital planning and investment controls (Office of Management and Budget/ property/asset management)

- Trail trace and tread management

- Visual Resource Management objectives

- Trail-specific Best Management Practices, including energy and minerals, livestock grazing, riparian, watershed, fisheries, wildlife, recreation, wilderness, lands and realty, etc.

- Signing and logo use

- National Scenic and Historic Trail use permits

- Exotic and invasive plant species

- Fire management rehabilitation

- Realty issues (easements–acquisitions–disposal)

- Comprehensive travel management (this includes all forms of motorized and nonmotorized access or use, such as foot, equestrian, mountain bike, off-highway vehicle, and other forms of transportation)

- Auto tour routes for historic trails

- Cultural Resources: Section 106/110 of the National Historic Preservation Act

- Section 7 of the Endangered Species Act

- Section 7 of the Wild and Scenic River Act

- Certification of eligible non-Federal sites and segments

- Conformance with Land Use Plans

- Trail corridor concept and planning area parameters

- Health and Safety/Hazards (e.g., hazardous waste, industrial areas, unsafe structures, hot springs, natural disasters, and others)

- Accessibility and Universal Design

- Interim Management between designation and Comprehensive Management Plan completion

- Interpretation, education, and public outreach—including interpretation of any or all of BLM's multiple-use functions along trails

6. Develop Training. Develop training for managers, staff specialists, and partners, which would emphasize on-the-ground trail management and understanding of the newly developed trail manual or handbook. Participate in the development of training and training aids (e.g., Internet sites) with the National Training Center for the National Trails System in collaboration with other agencies and partners.

- Training could include: Recreation Opportunity Spectrum, Limits of Acceptable Change, Visual Resource Management, Benefits Based Management, Best Management Practices, monitoring protocols, desired future conditions, and application of National Register of Historic Places criteria.

Objective 2: Ensure National Scenic and Historic Trail management is addressed within the Bureau's planning system.

Rationale: The integration of the unique management goals and needs of National Scenic and Historic Trails into the Bureau's planning process will identify the scope and condition of trail resources and prioritize on-the-ground solutions for sustained use and protection.

Actions:

1. Document Trail Resources. Inventory, assess, and evaluate National Scenic and Historic Trails.

- Use current data standards (including Interagency Trail Data Standards), performance measures, or other methodologies, ensuring that a data repository is created and maintained.

- Gather trail corridor and boundary data, including historic settings and high potential sites and segments where applicable. Share data with State Historic Preservation Offices in accordance with the National Historic Preservation Act.

- Establish a trail centerline and any associated zones using spatial technology for baseline documentation. Continue cooperation and coordination with other agencies and trail partners, as appropriate. Create a process for identifying and prioritizing cadastral survey services.

- Update or develop detailed historic context studies for National Historic Trails, which identify on-the-ground trail resources and condition of specific sites and segments.

- Identify trails as property management assets, capital planning, investment controls, and related issues, as required by the engineering program.

2. Determine Level of Planning Needed. Determine level of planning needed and required

for each NSHT (refer to BLM Planning Handbook Appendix C). Ensure conformance with Resource Management Plans, amendments, or generate amendments as needed. Involve respective partners. Ensure plans meet congressional intent of the specific Act and departmental guidance; e.g., National Trails System Act (Sections 5(e) and 5(f)) and amendments.

3. Prepare Management Plan Where Required or Necessary. Prepare guidance and develop plans as required or needed. Consider the following:

- Plan Integration Among Trail Agencies. Determine the relations among the various planning levels within the National Trails System (Comprehensive Management Plans for each National Scenic and Historic Trail, Resource Management Plans, activity plans at the State and field levels (e.g. travel management plans), and State Historic Preservation Plans developed by State Historic Preservation Offices). Provide direction for the integration of plans along the trails.

- Examine Use of Resource Allocation Tools. Identify and quantify trail resources and address how they fit into the following: Recreation Opportunity Spectrum, Visual Resource Management, accessibility or universal design, high potential sites and segments, cultural resource use categories, site-specific condition assessments, National Register of Historic Places eligibility, and others. Include the identification of trail trace or tread and trail management corridors in trail management plans.

- Examine Use of Special Designations. To enhance resource allocation determinations in planning under the multiple-use mandate, examine the use of special management areas along trails (e.g., Areas of Critical Environmental Concern and Special Recreation Management Areas). Consider withdrawals or lease and permit stipulations as management tools.

- Develop Trail-Specific Communication Plan. Develop a communication plan for each National Scenic and Historic Trail. Involve partners while analyzing and defining interest, funding, and commitment levels for the development and long-term management of interpretive centers. Identify timeframes, key messages, target audiences, and communication tools.

- Monitor Trail Resources. Include an inventory and monitoring program in trail management plans that uses current data standards. With partners, define conflicting use areas, separate inappropriate overlap, and educate public on revised use plan. Engage partners, stakeholders, and volunteers in use regulation and monitoring of trails, as appropriate.

4. Develop Business Plans for BLM-Administered Trails. For each BLM-administered trail, trail administrators with partners will develop a multiyear business plan. It should, at a minimum, consider:

- Marketing strategy plans

- Potential need for or existing visitor and interpretive centers

- Funding or partnership funding

- Challenge Cost-Share–Assistance Agreements–Memorandums of Understanding

- Grants training, development

- Stewardship programs

- Use fees

- Federal Highway Administration (surface transportation funding programs)

Partnership Goal

Engage and encourage partnership involvement in planning, development, maintenance, and management, where appropriate.

Objective 1: Maintain and enhance the Bureau's relation with trails partners.

Rationale: Congress, through legislation, continues to recognize the importance of partners and their contributions in the management and administration of National Scenic and Historic Trails. Partners can include: Federal, Tribal, State, and local agencies, local communities, advocates, organizations, stakeholders, and volunteers. Building common ground captures the unique synergy among partners in the National Trails System and encourages innovative approaches to trail management challenges and opportunities.

Actions:

1. Review and Update Partnership Guidance. Review existing partnership guidance and extract relevant elements. Enhance guidance to meet the unique needs of the National Scenic and Historic Trails Program. Consider status as trail cooperating associations.

2. Publish Initial NSHT Program Toolbox. This toolbox could include updated Partnership Guidance document, Federal Advisory Council Act rules and regulations, manuals and handbooks, toolbox of guidelines, forms, reporting expectations and format, outlines for general actions, limits to responsibilities, acceptable means of recognition, and downloadable format; include an appendix with examples of ineffective and effective partnerships utilizing Partners Case Studies.

3. Maintain or Establish Agreements. Identify existing Memorandums of Understanding (MOUs), agreements, and protocols. Continue or develop, as needed, key MOUs, agreements, or protocols among partners.

4. Develop an External Communication Plan. Trail staff and managers will use a communication plan to open channels among national, regional, State, local, and stakeholders. Ensure consistency with communication plan associated with the Administrative Goal. Items in the communication plan may include:

- A Web site that includes BLM trail-related staff (titles and their contact information), as well as partnership information (partner contact information, mission statements, trail relationship histories, and current activities).

- Link to the National Landscape Conservation System Web site.

- Identification of specific BLM managers for each partner to facilitate dialogues between Bureau offices.

- Additional public relations activities.

5. Engage in Regularly Scheduled Meetings. The BLM will participate in regularly scheduled meetings with trail partners, interested parties, and other agencies to discuss National Trail issues in an organized forum. Recommended annually.

6. Establish Advisory Councils or Charters, as needed. Where legislation calls for advisory councils on trails the agency administers, the BLM will advocate for their establishment. Where BLM manages—but does not administer—trail lands, BLM Resource Advisory Councils subgroups may be utilized for specific issues. All councils will be in compliance with the Federal Advisory Committee Act. The BLM will also advocate for the establishment of interagency charters and recommend a leadership council through a charter for each National Scenic and Historic Trail (e.g., the Continental Divide National Scenic Trail Charter).

7. Seek New Partnerships and Volunteers. Create innovative new partnerships with similar goals and expectations (e.g., State public education departments). Support volunteerism at all levels of

participation, through sponsors, in-kind donations, and hands-on activities to promote stewardship and common goals.

8. Solicit Involvement of Interested and Affected Publics in Resource Planning. For national trails and interpretive centers, build into all stages of planning, from the preplan forward, the expectation of inclusion of interested and affected publics.

9. Provide Opportunities for Partnership Involvement and Funding Opportunities in Plan Implementation, where appropriate. Build into operations and maintenance participation opportunities for partners. Opportunities may include: facilitating partner funding (e.g., private sector dollars and in-kind donations), use fee management, gift catalogues, education projects, resource maintenance, inventory and monitoring, private land ownership roles, third-party contracting, creative staffing, volunteerism, and trail stewards. Coordinate partnership opportunities with the Take Pride in America program.

Visitor Goal

Promote appropriate public access and foster visitor enjoyment, appreciation, and learning opportunities to provide for enriching and inspiring experiences.

Objective 1: Incorporate resource management techniques in the planning process to enhance the visitor experience along National Scenic and Historic Trails.

Rationale: Appropriate public access can be determined by incorporating resource management tools and techniques, which will allow the Bureau to make informed and defensible resource allocation decisions and provide for sustainable visitor use and resource protection.

Actions:

1. Incorporate Resource Allocation Tools. Emphasize the inclusion of resource allocation tools (e.g., recreation, cultural, engineering, and others) in the planning and management processes, such as: Limits of Acceptable Change, cultural resource use categories, monitoring protocols, carrying capacity, benefits-based management, Recreation Opportunity Spectrum, Visual Resource Management, and accessibility or universal design in the planning process.

2. Address Comprehensive Travel Management (this includes all forms of motorized and nonmotorized access or use, such as foot, equestrian, mountain bike, off-highway vehicle and other forms of transportation). Address comprehensive travel management issues in the planning process to provide for appropriate public access, use conflict avoidance, and needed protection for trail resources.

Objective 2: Establish a consistent approach to permitting use along trails.

Rationale: Clarity and consistency in the special use permit process will reduce confusion for both BLM managers and visitors to BLM lands, leading to enhanced experiences and protected resources.

Actions:

1. Clarify Application of Permit Guidance in Policy. Clarify application of permit guidance for multijurisdictional permits along National Scenic and Historic Trails.

2. Incorporate the Permitting Process for Special Uses in Trail Plans. Where appropriate, apply consistent approaches for permitting use (e.g., Special Recreation Permits, Cultural Resource Use Permits) along each National Scenic and Historic Trail. New trail plans should incorporate the following:

- Required permits

- Identification of lead office to coordinate permits, if necessary

- Process for coordination

Objective 3: Promote recreation and learning opportunities through improved information access and interpretation.

Rationale: Improving information services fosters positive visitor experiences, connects people to their natural and cultural resources, and promotes trail stewardship.

Actions:

1. Ensure Consistent Thematic Interpretation. Ensure consistent interpretation of trail themes along jurisdictional boundaries by developing an education and interpretive plan for each trail or significant trail segment. Use themes determined in the Comprehensive Management Plans.

2. Improve Information Access. Improve availability and access to trail information with partners. Mechanisms for information dissemination include:

- Official Web site for each trail

- Digital library with a database of photos and documents

- Link to related educational and interpretive sites

- National advertising or marketing campaign

3. **Provide Education Opportunities.** Provide public education opportunities through interpretive materials and interactions that clarify concepts of resource protection and restoration, appropriate use, local support, partners' support, fee program objectives, permit requirements, and available recreation opportunities along trails.

4. **Integrate Trail Goals with Those of Visitor or Interpretive Centers.** Enhance recreation and learning opportunities by proactively supporting the integration of trail management goals in visitor or interpretive centers.

5. **Utilize Visitor Satisfaction Surveys.** Consider the use of visitor use and satisfaction surveys to monitor visitation, enhance recreation experiences, and protect trail resources.

Objective 4: Ensure that visitor safety issues are identified and addressed along National Scenic and Historic Trails.

Rationale: There is an expectation that BLM has taken proactive measures to manage risks to visitors. Such measures help to reduce accidents and injuries and subsequent tort claims.

Actions:

1. **Coordinate with Visitor Safety Programs.** Coordinate National Scenic and Historic Trails management with existing visitor safety activities under BLM programs. Programs such as Hazard Management and Resource Restoration, the Abandoned Mine Land Cleanup Program, and Facilities Management have components related to visitor safety that can assist, including funding and GIS data.

BLM National Scenic and Historic Trails Work Plan

The following Work Plan outlines each Goal, Objective, and Action in summary form. It also shows the assigned priority for each action (critical, important, ongoing, or as needed), fiscal year the action will be initiated, the office responsible for initiating the action, and offices requiring coordination work to enhance each product. The BLM will coordinate with partners where indicated in the Strategy, and as appropriate in the implementation of other actions in the Work Plan.

The Work Plan is a guide to ensure that all actions in the Strategy are tracked and completed within the next 10 years. Initiation dates for some actions may vary. Opportunities will arise calling for immediate work on some items, while others may be delayed to join other related initiatives, or some work items may be combined for greater efficiencies. Each fiscal year, an Implementation Plan will be prepared by the BLM National Trails Program Coordinator to track, assess, and ensure progress on the Work Plan.

BLM National Scenic and Historic Trails Work Plan

ADMINISTRATIVE GOAL: Institute and formalize the National Scenic and Historic Trails (NSHT) Program within the BLM pursuant to the National Trails System Act and our multiple-use mandate.

Objective	Action and Priority	Initiate Action (FY)	Initiating Office	Coordinating Office
Objective 1: Establish an administrative infrastructure focusing on NSHTs in the Bureau.	1. Assess Workforce. (Critical)	FY 2006	WO-172	SO/FO
	2. Establish Trail Expert Team. (Critical)	FY 2006	WO-172	SO/FO
	3. Examine Visitor or Interpretive Centers' Roles. (Important)	FY 2008	WO-250	WO-172
Objective 2: Establish budget structure and improve funding stream for NSHTs in the Bureau.	1. Propose Need for Subactivity Account. (Critical)	FY 2006	WO-172	WO-880
	2. Propose Budget Themes for Budget Planning System. (Critical)	FY 2006	WO-172	WO-880
	3. Evaluate Need to Earmark Challenge Cost Share Themes for Funding Allocations. (Critical)	FY 2007	WO-172	WO-880
	4. Create Project Codes. (Important)	As needed	WO-172	WO-880
	5. Refine Performance Measures. (Ongoing)	As needed	WO-172	WO-880
Objective 3: Clarify and open communication channels within the administrative structure	1. Develop an Internal Communication Plan. (Critical)	FY 2007	WO-172	WO-610/250/240/FO/SO

RESOURCE GOAL: Protect and sustain trail resources to provide for enriching and inspiring experiences, scenic landscapes, and historic settings.

Objective	Action and Priority	Initiate Action (FY)	Initiating Office	Coordinating Office
Objective 1: Establish and implement national policy and guidance to identify and protect trail resources in conjunction with our multiple-use mandate.	1. Reconnect Trail Legislation to Contemporary Action. (Critical)	FY 2006	WO-172	WO-240/NPS/USFS
	2. Conduct Policy Review. (Critical)	FY 2007	WO-172	WO-630
	3. Consider Additional Regulations. (Important)	As needed	WO-172	WO-630/240/250/NPS/USFS/USFWS
	4. Develop National Register Bulletin. (Important)	FY 2008	WO-172	NPS/DOI/WO-240
	5. Develop Manuals or Handbooks. (Critical)	FY 2009	WO-172	WO-240/250
	6. Develop Training. (Critical-primer; Important-other)	Primer FY 2007 Then as needed	WO-172	NTC/240/250/360
Objective 2: Ensure NSHT management is addressed within the Bureau's planning system.	1. Document Trail Resources. (Critical)	FY 2006	FO	SO/WO-172
	2. Determine Level of Planning Needed. (Important)	FY 2008	FO/SO/WO-172	WO-210/250/240
	3. Prepare Management Plan Where Required or Necessary. (Important)	As needed	FO/SO	WO-210/172
	4. Develop Business Plans for BLM-Administered Trails. (Critical)	FY 2007	SO	FO/NPS/USFS/USFWS

PARTNERSHIP GOAL: Engage and encourage partner involvement in the planning, development, maintenance, and management, where appropriate.				
Objective	Action and Priority	Initiate Action (FY)	Initiating Office	Coordinating Office
Objective 1: Maintain and enhance the Bureau's relationship with trails partners.	1. Review and Update Partnership Guidance. (Critical)	FY 2006	WO-170	WO-172/240/250/650/DOI/NPS/ USFS/USFWS
	2. Publish Initial NSHT Program Toolbox. (Critical)	FY 2007	WO-172	WO-250/650/240
	3. Maintain or Establish Agreements. (Critical)	As needed	FO/SO/WO-172	WO-850
	4. Develop an External Communication Plan. (Important)	FY 2009	WO-172	WO-610/250/240/FO/SO/NPS/ USFS/USFWS
	5. Engage in Regularly Scheduled Meetings. (Important)	Annually	WO-172/SO/ FO	WO-240/250
	6. Establish Advisory Councils or Charters, as needed. (Important)	As needed	SO	WO-172/FO
	7. Seek New Partnerships and Volunteers. (Ongoing)	As needed	WO-650/SO/ FO	WO-172/240/250
	8. Solicit Involvement of Interested and Affected Publics in Resource Planning. (Ongoing)	FY 2006	FO/SO	WO-172/210/250
	9. Provide Opportunities for Partnership Involvement and Funding Opportunities in Plan Implementation, where appropriate. (Ongoing)	FY 2006	FO	SO/WO-172/170

VISITOR GOAL: Promote appropriate public access and foster visitor enjoyment, appreciation, and learning opportunities to provide for enriching and inspiring experiences.

Objective	Action and Priority	Initiate Action (FY)	Initiating Office	Coordinating Office
Objective 1: Incorporate resource management techniques in the planning process to enhance the visitor experience along NSHTs.	1. Incorporate Resource Allocation Tools. (Ongoing)	FY 2006	FO	SO/WO-172/250/240
	2. Address Comprehensive Travel Management. (Critical)	FY 2006	FO	SO/WO-172/250
Objective 2: Establish a consistent approach to permitting use along trails.	1. Clarify Application of Permit Guidance in Policy. (Critical)	FY 2009	WO-240/250	WO-172
	2. Incorporate the Permitting Process for Special Uses in Trail Plans. (Important)	FY 2006	WO-240/250	WO-172
Objective 3: Promote recreation and learning opportunities through improved information access and interpretation.	1. Ensure Consistent Thematic Interpretation. (Ongoing)	FY 2007	FO/WO-250	SO/WO-172
	2. Improve Information Access. (Critical)	FY 2007	FO/SO/WO-172	WO-650
	3. Provide Education Opportunities. (Critical)	As needed	FO/WO-650	WO-240/250/172
	4. Integrate Trail Goals with Those of Visitor and Interpretive Centers. (Critical)	FY 2008	FO/WO-250/172	SO
	5. Utilize Visitor Satisfaction Surveys. (Ongoing)	As needed	FO	WO-172/250/SO
Objective 4: Ensure that visitor safety issues are identified and addressed along NSHTs.	1. Coordinate with Visitor Safety Programs. (Ongoing)	FY 2006	WO-360	WO-250/172/SO/FO

Office Code Key

FO: BLM Field Office
SO: BLM State Office
WO: BLM Washington Office

WO-170: National Landscape Conservation System
WO-172: Wilderness, Rivers, and National Trails
WO-210: Planning, Assessment, and Community
WO-240: Cultural, Fossil Resources, and Tribal Consultation
WO-250: Recreation

WO-360: Protection and Response (engineering and hazardous materials)
WO-610: Public Affairs
WO-650: Environmental Education and Volunteers
WO-850: Property, Acquisition, and Headquarter Services
WO-880: Budget

Appendix A. Glossary.

Auto Tour Routes: Official driving route established for recreational touring within National Historic Trail corridors.

Comprehensive Management Plan: Statutorily required plan produced by the Trail Administering Agency in cooperation with Federal, Tribal, State, and local agencies, local communities, advocates, organizations, stakeholders, or volunteers.

Comprehensive Travel Management: Planning for all forms of motorized and nonmotorized access or use, such as foot, equestrian, mountain bike, off-highway vehicle and other forms of transportation.

Cooperating Agencies: Term used by the Council on Environmental Quality and supplemental BLM planning regulations for Federal, Tribal, State, and local agencies involved with the Bureau during the land use planning process.

Federal Land Policy and Management Act: The legislation that gave the Department of the Interior Bureau of Land Management (BLM) its mandate to manage public lands and natural resources for the benefit of all Americans. It consolidated and articulated BLM's management responsibilities by establishing, amending, or repealing many land and resource management authorities. FLPMA proclaimed multiple use, sustained yield, and environmental protection as the guiding principles for public land management.

High Potential Historic Segments: Those segments of a trail that would afford high-quality recreation experience in a portion of the route having greater than average scenic values or affording an opportunity to vicariously share the experience of the original users of a historic route (National Trails System Act, 16 U.S.C. 1241–1251).

High Potential Historic Sites: Those historic sites related to the route, or sites in close proximity thereto, which provide opportunity to interpret the historic significance of the trail during the period of its major use. Criteria for consideration as high potential sites include historic significance, presence of visible historic remnants, scenic quality, and relative freedom from intrusion (National Trails System Act, 16 U.S.C. 1241–1251).

Multiple-use: The management of the public lands and their various resource values so that they are utilized in the combination that will best meet the present and future needs of the American people; making the most judicious use of the land for some or all of these resources or related services over areas large enough to provide sufficient latitude for periodic adjustments in use to conform to changing needs and conditions; the use of some land for less than all of the resources; a combination of balanced and diverse resource uses that takes into account the long-term needs of future generations for renewable and nonrenewable resources, including recreation, range, timber, minerals, watershed, wildlife, and fish; natural scenic, scientific, and historical values; and harmonious and coordinated management of the various resources without permanent impairment of the productivity of the land and the quality of the environment with consideration being given to the relative values of the resources and not necessarily to the combination of uses that will give the greatest economic return or the greatest unit output (FLPMA, 43 U.S.C. 1702, Sec. 103 [c]).

National Historic Trails: Follow as closely as possible and practicable the original trails or routes of travel of national historic significance…[and]… shall have as their purpose the identification and protection of the historic route and its historic remnants and artifacts for public use and enjoyment (National Trail System Act 16 U.S.C. 1241–1251).

National Scenic Trails: So located as to provide for maximum outdoor recreation potential and for the conservation and enjoyment of the nationally significant scenic, historic, natural, or cultural qualities of the areas through which such trails may pass (National Trail System Act 16 U.S.C. 1241–1251).

National Register of Historic Places: The Nation's official list of cultural resources worthy of preservation. Authorized under the National Historic Preservation Act of 1966 (16 U.S.C. 470, as amended), the National Register is part of a national program to coordinate and support public and private efforts to identify, evaluate, and protect historic and archaeological resources. Properties listed in the Register include districts, sites, buildings, structures, and objects that are significant in American history, architecture, archaeology, engineering, and culture. The National Register is administered by the National Park Service, which is part of the U.S. Department of the Interior.

National Register Bulletins: Provide guidance to document, evaluate, and nominate historically significant sites to the National Register of Historic Places. The bulletin series is divided into four sections: Basics, Property Types, Technical Assistance, and General Guidance.

Partners: Federal, Tribal, State, and local agencies, local communities, advocates, organizations, stakeholders, or volunteers operating under mutual agreement and interests with the BLM.

Performance Measures: Measurement for work achieved on the basis of provisions in the Department of Interior Strategic Plan.

Project Codes: Two-digit alpha codes indicating specific types of work the BLM conducts.

Workload Measures: Measurement for work achieved for each BLM project code.

Appendix B. Bureau of Land Management (BLM)
National Scenic and Historic Trails Mileage Table.

National Trail Name	Type	BLM State	Miles
Iditarod[1]	Historic	Alaska	418
Juan Bautista De Anza[2]	Historic	Arizona, California	116
California[2]	Historic	California, Idaho, Nevada Oregon, Utah, Wyoming	1,391
Nez Perce[3]	Historic	Idaho, Montana, Wyoming	70
Lewis and Clark[2]	Historic	Idaho, Montana	369
Pony Express[2]	Historic	Nevada, Utah, Wyoming	697
Oregon[2]	Historic	Idaho, Oregon, Wyoming	656
Mormon Pioneer[2]	Historic	Wyoming	213
El Camino Real de Tierra Adentro[4]	Historic	New Mexico, Texas	60
Old Spanish[4]	Historic	Arizona, California, Colorado, Nevada, New Mexico, Utah	887
Subtotal—Historic (10)			4,877
Continental Divide[3]	Scenic	Idaho, Montana, Colorado, New Mexico, Wyoming	377
Pacific Crest[3]	Scenic	California, Oregon	231
Subtotal—Scenic Trails (2)			608
Grand Total			5,485

[1] Trail administered by the BLM (Department of the Interior)
[2] Trail administered by the National Park Service (Department of the Interior)
[3] Trail administered by the U.S. Forest Service (Department of Agriculture)
[4] Trail coadministered by the BLM and the National Park Service (Department of the Interior)

Appendix C. Map of the Bureau of Land Management National Landscape Conservation System National Scenic and Historic Trails.

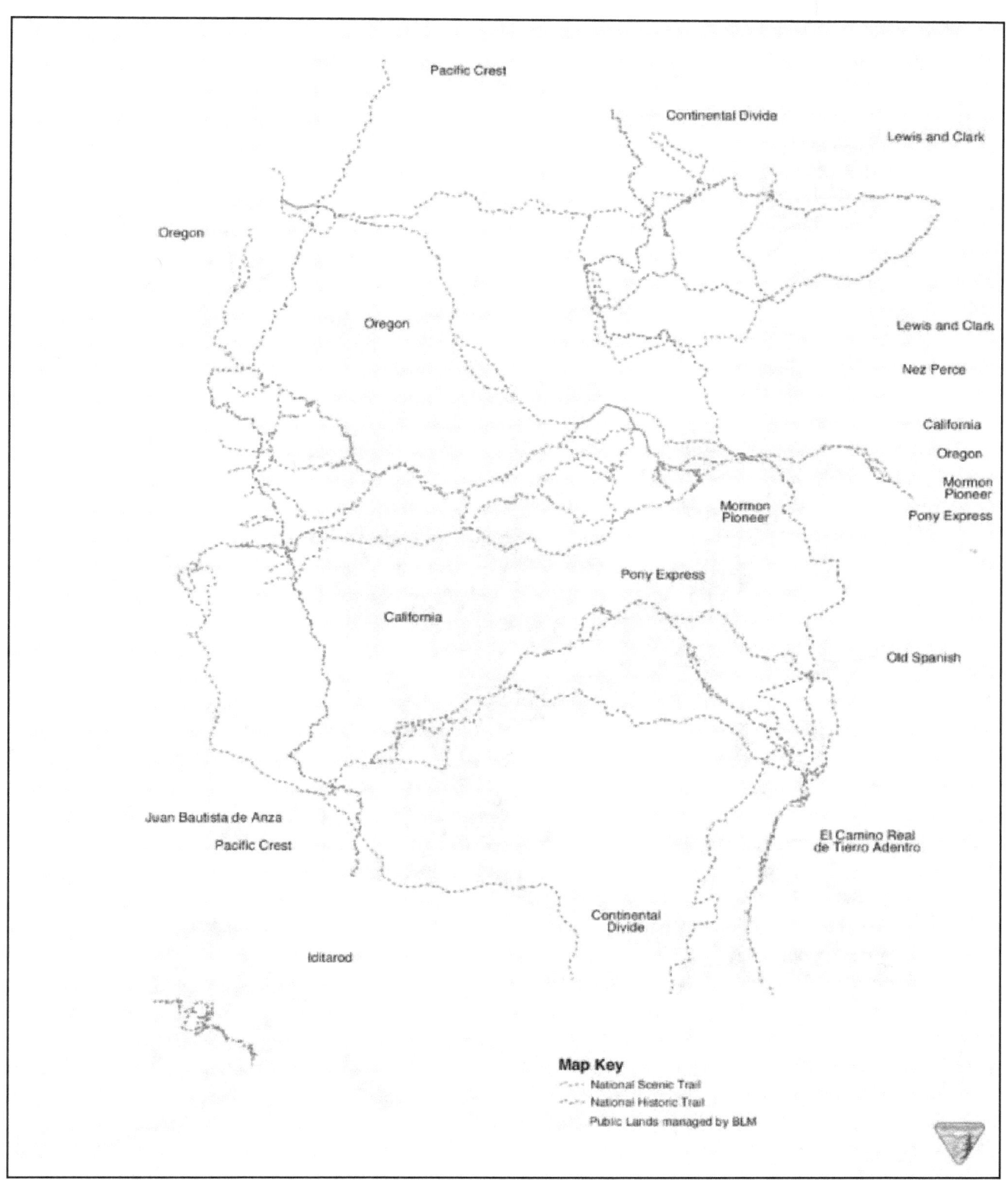

Editing, design, and layout provided by the
BLM National Science and Technology Center's Publishing Staff, Denver, Colorado.

www.ingramcontent.com/pod-product-compliance
Lightning Source LLC
Chambersburg PA
CBHW081135280526
45787CB00007B/3094